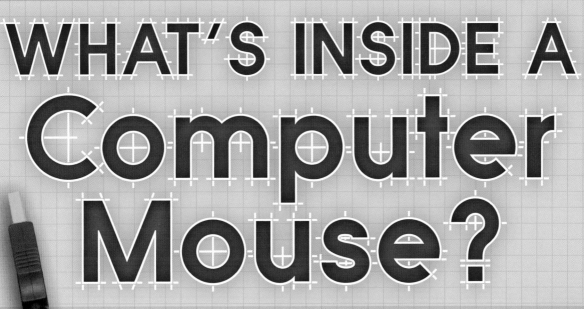

WHAT'S INSIDE A Computer Mouse?

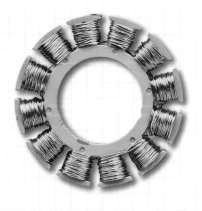

Published by The Child's World®
1980 Lookout Drive • Mankato, MN 56003-1705
800-599-READ • www.childsworld.com

Photographs ©: Rick Orndorf, cover (mouse), cover (mouse wheel), 1 (mouse), 1 (mouse wheel), 4, 7, 9, 11, 13 (mouse wheel) 13 (circuit board), 14, 15, 17 (green circuit board), 17 (brown circuit board), 19 (mouse), 19 (USB cable), 20; Shutterstock Images, cover (circuit board), 1 (circuit board), 2, 3 (circuit board), 3 (plug), 5 (scissors), 5 (safety glasses), 6, 8, 10, 12, 16, 18 (button), 18 (plug), 21, 22, 23, 24; Praiwun Thungsarn/Shutterstock Images, 3 (screwdriver), 5 (screwdriver), 8 (screwdriver); Shyripa Alexandr/Shutterstock Images, 5 (gloves)

ISBN 9781503832091
LCCN 2018962814

Printed in the United States of America
PA02419

About the Author

Arnold Ringstad lives in Minnesota.

He uses computer mice every day.

Contents

Materials and Safety

Materials

- ☐ Computer mouse
- ☐ Phillips screwdriver
- ☐ Safety glasses
- ☐ Scissors
- ☐ Work gloves

Safety

- Always be careful with sharp objects, such as screwdrivers.

- Unplug the mouse, and then cut the cord before you start.

- Wear work gloves to protect your hands from sharp edges.

- Wear safety glasses in case pieces snap off.

Computer Mouse

Important!

Be sure to get an adult's permission before taking anything apart. When you're taking things apart, have an adult nearby in case you need help or have questions.

Phillips
screwdriver

Work gloves

Scissors

Safety glasses

Inside a Mouse

People use a mouse with a
computer. They move the mouse
across a desk. This moves a **cursor**
on the computer screen. People
can click things on the screen. They
can use a wheel on the mouse
to **scroll** up and down. How
does a computer mouse work?
What's inside?

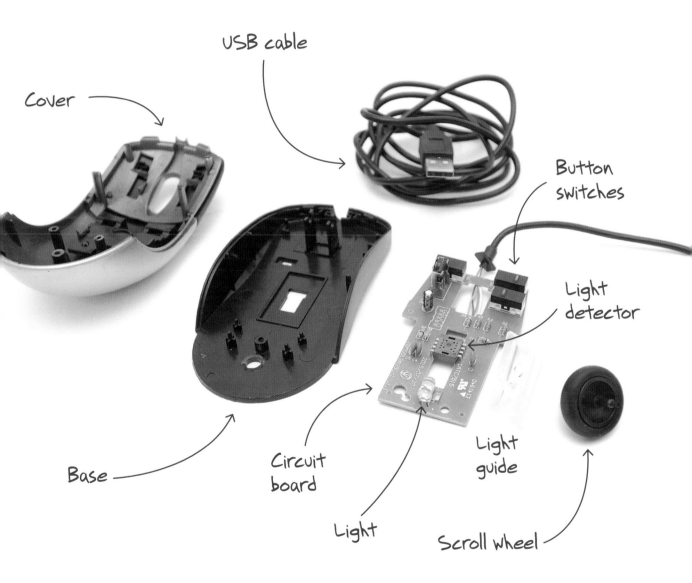

Cover

USB cable

Button switches

Light detector

Base

Circuit board

Light

Light guide

Scroll wheel

Opening the Mouse

First, unplug and cut the cord of the mouse for safety. Then, look at the bottom of the mouse. A screw may hold the mouse together. Use a Phillips screwdriver to remove it. The mouse cover will come off. You will see the **circuit board**.

Safety Note

Cut the cord a few inches away from the mouse.

Safety Note

Be careful not to

lose the screw.

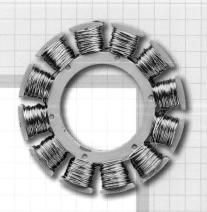

Clicking

The mouse buttons are on the cover. Pressing a button presses a switch below. Each button has its own switch. The switches make clicking sounds. The switches tell the computer that the user clicked a button.

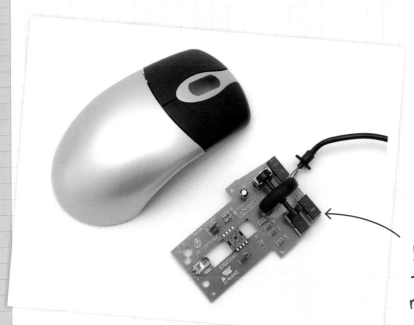

The mouse's buttons click these tiny red switches.

People click **icons** on computer screens. Clicking icons opens pictures, games, and other things on the computer.

Scrolling

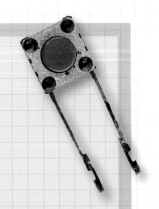

The mouse's wheel spins forward or backward. It tells the computer to scroll. This makes things on the computer screen move up or down. Users can press the wheel, too. This presses a switch below. Just like the buttons, the switch makes a clicking sound. Pull out the wheel to see the switch that it presses.

The mouse wheel rests on the circuit board.

Making a Light

There is a light on the circuit board.
It shines on the **light guide**.
This part reflects light downward.

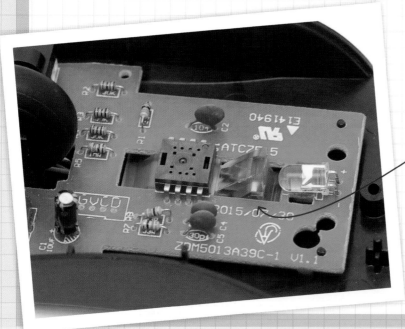

The light guide
is shaped like
a triangle.

The light travels through the hole on the bottom of the mouse.

The light goes through a hole in the bottom of the mouse. It hits the flat surface below, usually a desk or mouse pad. It creates a pattern of light. Pull the circuit board off the base. Remove the light guide, too.

Safety Note

The circuit board may have sharp points. Be sure to wear work gloves.

Seeing the Light

The circuit board has a **light detector**. It is like a simple camera. The light pattern changes as the mouse moves. The detector sees these changes. It tells the computer to move the cursor. The cursor moves across the screen as the user pushes the mouse around.

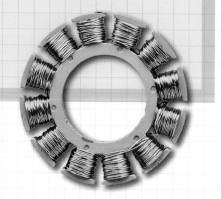

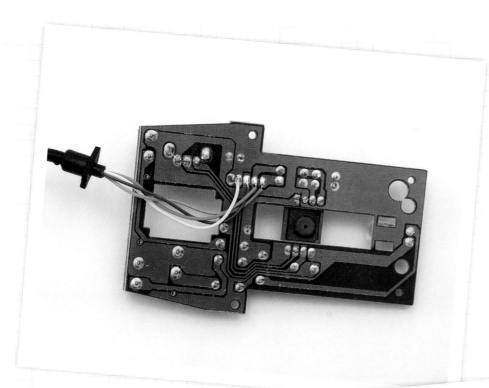

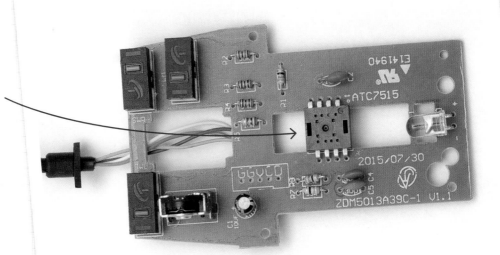

Top of
light detector

The USB Cable

The mouse talks to the computer through the mouse cord. The cord is called a USB cable. One end goes into the mouse. Wires attach to the circuit board. The other end fits in the computer. The cable gives the mouse power. It also carries information to the computer.

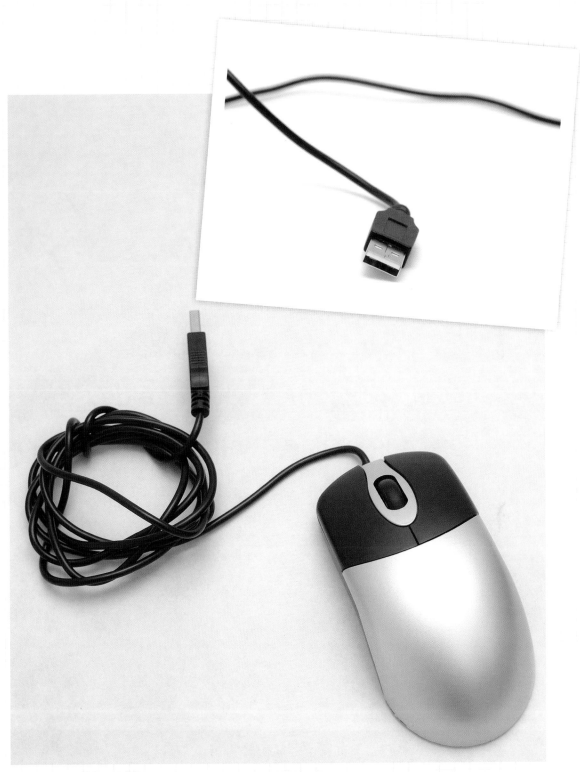

USB cables are used to connect mice and keyboards to computers.

Reusing a
Computer Mouse

We've taken apart a computer
mouse and learned what's inside.
Now what? Here are some ideas
for how to reuse the parts of a
computer mouse. Can you think of
any more?

- **Make a Top**: Stand the scroll wheel up on one end and spin it!

- **Clicking Code**: Use the switches to make clicking sounds. Invent a code and send messages to friends in a quiet room.

- **Mouse-y Bank**: Take the circuit board out of the mouse, then put the top back on. Drop coins through the scroll wheel hole to use the mouse as a piggy bank!

Glossary

circuit board (SUR-kit BORD): A circuit board is a piece of material that holds computer chips, switches, and other parts. The mouse has a circuit board inside.

cursor (KUR-sur): A cursor is a small shape on a computer screen that shows where the mouse is pointing. Moving the mouse moves the cursor.

icon (EYE-kon): An icon is a picture on a computer screen that stands for something. Clicking on an icon will open a program or file.

light detector (LITE di-TEK-tur): A light detector is a part that can see light in front of it. The mouse's light detector lets it see how patterns of light change on the table below.

light guide (LITE GIDE): A light guide is a piece of plastic that reflects light in a certain way. The mouse's light guide reflects light downward through the bottom of the mouse.

scroll (SKROHL): To scroll is to shift something up or down on a computer. The mouse's wheel lets users scroll through things on their computers.

To Learn More

IN THE LIBRARY

Koontz, Robin. *Computer Mouse*. Vero Beach,
FL: Rourke Educational Media, 2015.

Robinson, Peg. *How Computers Work*.
New York, NY: Cavendish Square, 2019.

Zuchora-Walske, Christine. *What's Inside My Computer?*
Minneapolis, MN: Lerner Publishing Group, 2016.

ON THE WEB

Visit our website for links about taking apart a
computer mouse: **childsworld.com/links**

Note to Parents, Teachers, and Librarians: We routinely verify our Web links to make sure they
are safe and active sites. So encourage your readers to check them out!

Index